THE BASIC NEW MEXICO
B**U**CKET
LIST

100 Things to Do in New Mexico Before You Die
by Barbe Awalt

Río Grande Books
Los Ranchos, NM

Río Grande Books

The Bucket List Book Series

The Basic New Mexico Bucket List by Barbe Awalt
Release – Summer of 2015

The Complete Hot Air Balloon Bucket List by Barbe Awalt
Release – Fall 2015

The Complete Cowboy Bucket List by Slim Randles
Release – Winter of 2015

The Complete Shopping Bucket List by Barbe Awalt
Release – Spring 2016

The Complete Space Buff Bucket List by Loretta Hall
Release – Spring 2016

Copyright © 2015 Barbe Awalt

Published by Río Grande Books
925 Salamanca NW, Los Ranchos, NM 87107-5647
505-344-9382   www.LPDPress.com

Printed in the United States of America
Book Design: Paul Rhetts

Library of Congress Cataloging-in-Publication Data

Awalt, Barbe.
The Ultimate New Mexico bucket list : 100 things to do in New
Mexico before you die / by Barbe Awalt.
pages cm
ISBN 978-1-936744-25-1 (paperback : alk. paper)
1. New Mexico--Guidebooks. 2. New Mexico--Description and
travel. I. Title.
F794.3.A93 2015
917.8904--dc23
2015000927

*Front cover: ©Scukrov-Bucket and ©Iivanovich1-Zia Symbol, Dreamstime.
com; Back cover: Albuquerque International Balloon Fiesta and chiles,
Courtesy New Mexico True, New Mexico Department of Tourism.*

CONTENTS

Gran Quivira ruins. Courtesy New Mexico True, New Mexico Department of Tourism.

Entrance to Sparky's Restaurant, Hatch, New Mexico. Courtesy Barbe Awalt.

The Bucket List

We visited New Mexico many times in the early 1980s. We liked it so much we moved here permanently from Maryland in 1990. The first thing you have to do in New Mexico is visit and experience everything. It is a very unpredictable place with a colorful history and unusual customs. New Mexico is a very different place—that is why it is exciting.

This book is a celebration of everything New Mexico. Everyone's bucket list is different, but these are the "basic" items and many are items that have made New Mexico famous. The order is not all that important but I do believe that chile is #1. Of course, you can add your own items, and if something is not on my list it does not reflect badly on it. It is a place to start exploring and find out if you have seen all that New Mexico has to offer. Remember, New Mexico is like coming to a foreign country—but you can drink the water in most places!

Seeing a recent show on TV brought back to me that many people in the USA do not think New Mexico is part of the USA. I even had a clerk at a store in Boston say she didn't accept checks written on banks in foreign countries. Many people think you need to have a passport to come here and we use foreign currency. There is even a column in *New Mexico Magazine*—"One of Our Fifty Is Missing." It all makes us laugh.

If you see and experience all of New Mexico, it may help you understand why New Mexico is the way it is —good and bad.

Because this is a hi-tech kind of world, many of the entries have a website for more information. Research what you are interested in. Many of the websites have contacts to get more information. There is also a Near Miss section with some ideas submitted by Facebook followers.

Special thanks to New Mexico True: New Mexico Department of Tourism, National Radio Observatory, Tucumcari Chamber of Commerce, Paul Rhetts, John T. Denne, Don James, Rio Metro, Plein Art Painters of Southern New Mexico, James Blackburn—New Mexico Gunfighters Association, Kiwanis Club of Santa Fe, Russell Lee, Kokopelli Rafting Adventures, Jim Harris—Lea County Museum, Organ Peak Mountain Desert Peaks National Museum, Roadrunner Food Bank, and Loretta & Jerry Hall.

Tour de Gila Road Race, Courtesy New Mexico True, New Mexico Department of Tourism.

In every *Bucket List* book we have a charity in the back of the book, and this is no exception. The Road Runner Food Bank is this book's hope to help.

Make your own bucket list – use this for a guide to do your own!

Clown-n-Around Brazil balloon at the 1995 Albuquerque International Balloon Fiesta, Albuquerque. Courtesy Barbe Awalt.

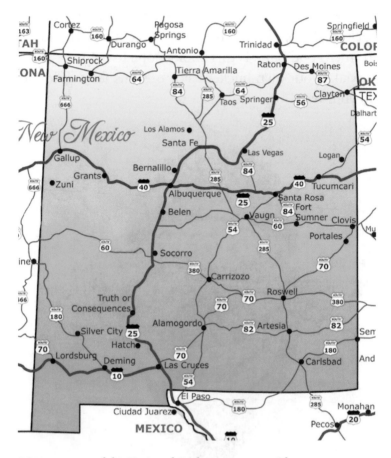

Map courtesy of the National Radio Astronomy Observatory.

The List

100. Buy a Cowboy Hat & Bandanna

You need a hat and bandanna for all the other items in the list. They protect against sun, rain, and wind. Get a great hat at the Men's Hat Shop on Central in Albuquerque, Old Town Hat Shop, or at O'Farrell Hat Company, Hatsmith, Davis Hats, and Montecristi Hats in Santa Fe. There are summer hats and wool, winter hats. There are decorative hats and utilitarian hats. Bandannas or rags are everywhere in every color! If you want a worn hat, try a flea market or second hand store.—www.travelandleisure.com/santafehats.

Cowboy hats at Sheplers, Albuquerque. Courtesy Barbe Awalt.

99. Eat Something Piñon

Piñon coffee, candy, foods, wine, incense, and anything else you can think of are available in New Mexico. Try harvesting piñon nuts. Take home piñon candy or coffee as souvenirs. You can find an assortment of piñon products in the New Mexico section of any grocery store. Of course you can just eat the nuts – native New Mexicans love them.—www.motherearthnews.com/pinonnuts.

New Mexico Piñon Coffee. Courtesy Barbe Awalt.

98. Explore Tucumcari

There is so much to see in Tucumcari. The best place I experienced was the Tucumcari Mountain Cheese Factory on East Main Street. I bought some flavors of cheese to take home. Yes, they have green chile cheese flavor and now have organic cheese. TMCF is an award-winning cheese maker. Mesalands Community College's Dinosaur Museum is very cool.—www.tucumcarinm.com.

Route 66 Monument at Sunset. Courtesy Tucumcari Chamber of Commerce.

97. Take a Picture of a Sunset

Every day you have an opportunity to take a picture that is an AHH! With our great landscapes and settings, they can all be individual. Tweet them out to friends if they have not-so-good weather. Make them angry. The best colors in a sunset are after a storm or during a fire —dust in the air. Don't forget sunrises too! And by the way, we have great clouds too!

Sandia sunset. Courtesy New Mexico True, New Mexico Department of Tourism.

96. Ski Santa Fe, Sandia, Angel Fire, Sipapu, Red River, Pajarito, Ski Apache, or Taos

When we have snow, we have great skiing. Stay in a hotel nearby and curl up next to a roaring fire. If you don't know how to ski, take a class. Eat at a fun and funky place. Shop in your down time. Make a vacation out of skiing.—www.skinewmexico.com.

Skiing in Taos. Courtesy New Mexico True, New Mexico Department of Tourism.

95. Ride the Chama Railroad

Chama has great weather in the summer, when it is hot everywhere else. It is in the mountains. In the winter Chama can get dumped on with monumental snow. Do ride the Cumbres & Toltec Railroad. They have ½ day trains and full day adventures. The landscape is spectacular, especially when the trees are turning colors. Stay in Chama in a mountain cabin.—www.cumbrestoltec.com.

Cumbres & Toltec Railroad, Chama. Courtesy New Mexico True, New Mexico Department of Tourism.

94. Eat Tamales, Posole, Calabacitas, Indian Tacos, Green Chile Stew, Sopapillas, Burritos, Enchiladas, Carne Adovado & Asada, Chile, and Chili & Beans

We have great food in New Mexico from the traditions of Hispanics, Native Americans, and cowboys. When you are outside at a pueblo, festival, or sightseeing, the food always tastes better. Everyone has their favorite place to eat if they don't have a great cook in the family. The Tamal Fiesta y Más in Silver City celebrates the food everyone likes — tamales. There is nothing like a bowl of green chile stew or posole when it is cold. There are chile festivals, a Bacon Fest, Coffee & Chocolate Festival, and many more. Eat until you explode.

Bueno Foods Sopaipilla mix. Courtesy Barbe Awalt.

93. Explore Chaco Canyon

Chaco Canyon is an international treasure and a step back into time. Chaco is between Farmington and Albuquerque. It is not an easy, quick drive. We are talking dirt roads. It is not a theme park with all kinds of conveniences. Campers are encouraged. The Night Sky Programs are legendary. Do your research, leave early, take provisions including water, and make sure you take a camera. Everyone takes the "doorway" picture, so take yours.—www.nps.gov/chcu/.

Chaco Canyon. Courtesy New Mexico True, New Mexico Department of Tourism.

92. Buy Some Turquoise

You can get turquoise on anything: jewelry, belt buckles, adorning clothes and vests, purses, furniture, art, frames, and much more. There are also many books on the history and beauty of turquoise. Visit a flea market to find some old or new turquoise—but make sure it is the real thing. Check that it is marked and from the USA—not China! There is a lot of fake turquoise and turquoise from China. If you drive up to Madrid or Cerrillos, you can see historic turquoise mines. The Native Americans found it, but we are all enjoying it. Visit the Turquoise Museum outside of Old Town Albuquerque.—www.turquoisemuseum.com.

If you are in the exploring mode, drive the Turquoise Trail National Scenic Byway. It is an easy one-day trip linking Santa Fe and Albuquerque.—www.turquoise-trail.org.

Turquoise. Courtesy New Mexico True, New Mexico Department of Tourism.

91. Visit Grants & Acoma Sky City

Grants is an old mining and uranium town that may be reborn. The Ice Cave is great when you have had enough of hot weather. You don't want an extended stay there in the prisons. Grants is on the way to Gallup on I-40. On the way to Grants is Acoma Sky City. Do take the tour up. It is breathtaking. Learn about the history of Acoma and see Native Americans selling pots. Take time to go in the new Acoma Cultural Center.—www.grants.org; www.acomaskycity.org.

Acoma Pueblo. Courtesy New Mexico True, New Mexico Department of Tourism.

90. Shop at a Flea Market

There are many flea markets in New Mexico and they can be fun. We have gotten a puppy and jewelry at the "Flea" market in Santa Fe. Both purchases were not planned. You can also take great pictures at a flea market. There can be stolen goods for sale, so beware. Not all flea markets are open all week, so do check the hours as well as the location.—www.fleaportal.com/newmexico.

Flea Market sign. Courtesy Barbe Awalt.

89. Visit Lincoln

Smokey Bear is a cultural icon. He is an American Black Bear who got caught in the Capitan Gap Fire in the Lincoln National Forest in 1950 as a small cub. Smokey was flown to the National Zoo in Washington DC. Smokey died in 1976 and his remains were returned to New Mexico. Please do not use "the" in the name because it is so incorrect. It was a song thing. The Ad Council campaign to prevent forest fires actually began in 1944, but in 1950 they got a real live bear who lived through a massive fire.—www.smokeybear.com.

The town of Lincoln is the site of the famous Lincoln County Wars. Billy the Kid, Pat Garrett, and other infamous people lived in the 17 historic structures that are part of the site. There is an admission charge.—www.nmhistoricsites.org/lincoln.

Billy the Kid tintype. Courtesy Organ Mountains Desert Peaks National Monument.

88. Play at a Casino

We are blessed or cursed with great casinos all over New Mexico – over twenty of them. Some are large and Las Vegas-like, and some are small and intimate. My favorites are: Inn of the Mountain Gods in Ruidoso, Buffalo Thunder Resort north of Santa Fe, and Rt. 66 Casino and Sandia Casino—both in Albuquerque. But there are also Isleta, Taos, Ohkay, Santa Clara, Camel Rock, Cities of Gold, Dancing Eagle, Fire Rock, The Downs, Zia Park, Billy the Kid, Casino Hollywood, Santa Ana, Wild Horse, Sunland, Sun Ray, and Sky City. I have favorites because—thank God—I don't live near all of them! Besides slots, bingo, and poker, the casinos have great places to eat and bring in top names doing shows. The casinos also have specialty shows. Some have spas, swimming pools, golf courses, clubs, and hotels.

Sandia Casino. Courtesy Paul Rhetts.

87. Eat Your Way Through the Green Chile Cheeseburger Trail

Each State Fair, the winner of the Best Green Chile Cheeseburger is crowned in a taste test. Who is the best? If you go on the Green Chile Cheeseburger Trail website from New Mexico Tourism, you can find the best places to eat all over New Mexico. Everybody has green chile on their burger – even the fast food chains. Those are good eats!—www.newmexico.org/green-chile-cheese-burger.

Green chile cheeseburger. Courtesy New Mexico True, New Mexico Department of Tourism.

86. Explore Silver City

Silver City is a funky town that will transport you to the past. I love the Silver City Museum, and the bed & breakfasts are fun places to stay. Silver City is one of the hosts of the Tour de Gila Bike Race in the spring and the Tamal Fiesta y Más in November. They are also known for the music and art scene. There are also some good eats in Silver City. The pottery exhibit at Western New Mexico University is a must see. Go to nearby Gila Cliff Dwellings. Check out the massive open mines at Chino or Tyrone. There are two ways to Silver City—the fast way through Hatch or the scenic and winding route through the mountains.—www.townofsilvercity.org.

North Bullard Street, Silver City. Courtesy Paul Rhetts.

85. Ride in a Pick-up Truck

Noted author Max Evans says he had the first pick-up truck in Taos, New Mexico, after World War II. Pick-up trucks are part of the New Mexico history because they are workhorses. On a ranch, in the ski areas, or as a city slicker, you need a pick-up truck. See how many pick-ups you see at the Balloon Fiesta hauling a gondola and envelope. Some of the best pictures are pick-up trucks with a full load of chiles in the fall.—www.american-cowboy.com.

Santa Fe pickup truck. Courtesy Barbe Awalt.

84. See Chimayó

The holy village of Chimayó hosts thousands of pilgrims during the Lenten Holy Week. Pilgrims also walk up Tomé Hill and in Las Cruces. When in Chimayó, you need to travel with a small ziplock to get your holy dirt. Yes, it is touted as the cure for a number of ailments. Around the holy dirt hole are many crutches from people who walked after using dirt. Get in the mood by seeing Robert Redford's *Milagro Beanfield War* on video—it was filmed around Truchas. The book was written by the great John Nichols of Taos. Locals have fun seeing it again and again because there are big names in the movie and we love to pick out New Mexicans that make a cameo.—www.elsantuariodechimayo.us.

El Santuario de Chimayó. Courtesy John T. Denne.

83. Visit the State Fair (Expo NM)

The State Fair/Expo of New Mexico is in Albuquerque starting after Labor Day. You can also visit a smaller fair in various counties all over New Mexico. State Fair in Albuquerque recently changed its name to Expo. It is a kinda dumb name and will probably change back. It is a State Fair and not an Expo. Expo or State Fair hosts many events all year from craft fairs to concerts and now has a modern casino—The Downs.—www.exponm.com.

Expo flags near The Downs. Courtesy Barbe Awalt.

82. Sample Some Lavender

We used to have a really big Lavender Festival in Los Ranchos, outside Albuquerque—not so much anymore. But there are good lavender fairs all over New Mexico. Do see the other crop in New Mexico. Take time to visit the Los Poblanos Farm Store on Rio Grande Blvd. in Los Ranchos for a crash course in what you can do with lavender—marshmallows, spices, seasoned nuts, hand cream, and much more. This is a family friendly setting that kids will love. Make sure to check out the peacocks. There is nothing better than lavender ice cream or lavender lemonade in summer.—www.lospoblanos.com.

Travelin' Jack and Jill Lane in Los Poblanos Lavender Fields. Courtesy Barbe Awalt.

81. Sun in Elephant Butte & T or C

Elephant Butte Lake is the closest thing we have to a beach. Every Memorial Day weekend and 4th of July, Elephant Butte is packed with campers, swimmers, or the not-so-hardy staying in hotels or rented homes. Elephant Butte is a stone's throw from T or C (Truth or Consequences). T or C, in Sierra County, was originally called Hot Springs for the water used in their spa treatments. In 1950, Ralph Edwards, the radio host, announced he would broadcast his radio show from the first town that renamed itself. So Truth or Consequences was born because of the radio show.—www.torcnm.org, http://cityofelephantbutte.com

Elephant Butte. Courtesy Paul Rhetts.

80. Explore the Four Corners, Shiprock & Farmington

When you visit Shiprock and the Four Corners, stay in Farmington, an oil/gas town with a Native American/western vibe. The sites are worth seeing, as is the Farmington Museum & Visitors Center at Gateway Park.—www.farmingtonnm.org.

To see Shiprock (Navajo for rock with wings) is awe inspiring. It has been used in movies and commercials. You need to take a picture of the iconic rock.

The Four Corners is near Shiprock and is the only place in the U. S. to have four states touch. You can stand in New Mexico, and touch Arizona, Utah, and Colorado. Visit the Monument.—www.navajonationparks.org/htm/fourcorners.htm

Shiprock. Courtesy Don James.

79. Explore the Navajo Reservation

The Navajo Reservation extends from New Mexico to Arizona and Utah, but boundaries are to be ignored. Do go to Window Rock and see the Navajo Nation Museum and rock foundations. I say "nation" because when you are on any reservation you are in a different country. Respect their culture and laws. Yes, The Navajo Nation Museum is in Arizona, but…—www.discover-navajo.com.

Road sign. Courtesy Don James, from One Nation One Year.

78. Experience a Pueblo Dance

There are dances for all seasons and for different sizes of gatherings. Dances are wonderful to view. Before you go, you need to see the accepted behaviors on the Indian Pueblo Cultural Center website. I have heard horror stories about phones with cameras being confiscated, so prepare in advance of going. While at any Pueblo, eat a Frito Pie. Go to the Indian Pueblo Cultural Center and find out more about where you are going. Do not be an ugly Anglo.

The best list of dances and feast days is at the Indian Pueblo Cultural Center.—www.indianpueblo.org.

Pueblo dance at the Indian Pueblo Cultural Center. Courtesy Barbe Awalt.

77. Ride in a Hot Air Balloon & More

Ballooning can be a dangerous sport, but only if the winds come up or you have a pilot that isn't experienced. It is like floating, and the rise into the skies is gentle. The landing may be a bit interesting. You see the land, animals, people, buildings and get a whole new perspective. The ultimate is a balloon ride from the field during Balloon Fiesta. Watch out for the christening afterwards! After your ride, you need to go the Anderson-Abruzzo Albuquerque International Balloon Museum to study and buy stuff. It is said, your first balloon ride is free and the next is $50,000 – for a new balloon. We hope you get an Albuquerque box or a splash 'n dash!—www.hotair-ballooning.com; www.balloonmuseum.com.

Albuquerque International Balloon Fiesta. Courtesy Barbe Awalt.

76. Take a Space Ride?

If you have been there and done that on balloon rides, then save your pennies for a space ride. For only $250,000 you get a ride in space on the Virgin Galactic space ship at the Spaceport America southeast of Truth or Consequences. Yes, a lot of people have actually signed up to go into space and paid a deposit. Two hours away, you can see the space stuff at the New Mexico Museum of Space History in Alamogordo.—www. spaceportamerican.com; www.nmspacemuseum.org.

Museum of Space History, Alamogordo. Courtesy New Mexico True, New Mexico Department of Tourism.

75. Ride the Sandia Tram

It is the longest tram in the world. You can see wildlife and go up to the observation store and platform. It is worth it to take tourists up, have a good meal, and see a wonderful sunset. Maybe you will be lucky and see a bear. There is a charge to ride the tram or enter the Sandia Tram area and park.—www.sandiapeak.com.

Sandia Tram. Courtesy New Mexico True, New Mexico Department of Tourism.

74. See a Roadrunner & Ride the Rail Runner

The greater roadrunner is the New Mexico bird. It is everywhere. Does it bring back cartoon memories? Avoid bears—they are not warm and fuzzy. Black bears are the official state mammal.—www.allaboutbirds.org/guide/Greater_Roadrunner.

Named after the roadrunner, the Rail Runner is a fast way to travel between Belen, Albuquerque, and Santa Fe; this is especially good when trying to attend things like Indian Market in Santa Fe. It is a wonderful experience and worth doing. Kids love it. We need more trains, mass transit, and transportation with experiences. During the holidays, there are special trains with themed entertainment.—www.riometro.org.

Railrunner. Courtesy Rio Metro.

73. Buy a New Mexico Book

This is one of the things I am passionate about. How can you find out about New Mexico unless you read about the art, culture, and history of New Mexico? Books make a great souvenir and kids love a New Mexico book. We have many great authors: Rudolfo Anaya, Fray Angelico Chavez, Don Bullis, Slim Randles, Tony and Anne Hillerman, Michael McGarrity, Father Tom Steele, Judith VanGeisen, John Nichols, Nasario Garcia, Max Evans, just to name a few. Visit with them! Did you know that *Ben Hur* was written by a New Mexican Governor? And before you write your own book, visit Bookworks, Treasure House, and Page One—my favorite bookstores in Albuquerque.—www.nmbookcoop.com; www.southwestwriters.com; www.nmbook.org.

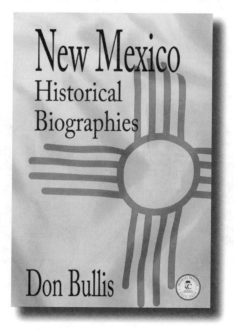

72. Go to Spanish Market & Buy a Santo

Spanish Market, the last full weekend in July, is the largest Hispanic Market in the world. Did you know there are actually two markets in the same place—Traditional Spanish Market and Contemporary Hispanic Market. Both are free, hot, filled with good art, and worth seeing.—www.spanishcolonial.org; www.contemporaryhispanicmarketinc.com.

A *santo* can protect from anything including bad neighbors, lightning, lost pets, and death. *Santos* are depictions of saints or items in the Catholic religion like crosses. *Santos* have been made in New Mexico for more than 400 years. They came from Mexico and Spain.

Contemporary Hispanic Market, Santa Fe. Courtesy Barbe Awalt.

71. Visit a New Mexico Museum

There are museums for art, history, cars, individual areas, culture, science, agriculture, Native Americans, and so much more. My favorites: The Los Lunas Museum of Art & Heritage, Silver City Museum, Albuquerque Museum, and New Mexico History Museum-it has to be–we are in it!—www.newmexicoculture.org.

National Hispanic Cultural Center courtyard. Courtesy New Mexico True, New Mexico Department of Tourism.

70. Explore Las Cruces

Las Cruces has so much to offer—great weather, New Mexico State University, good food, and proximity to Mexico. I love the New Mexico Farm & Ranch Museum. Cowboy Days are a crowd pleaser at the Farm & Ranch Museum in March. Go in January and laugh at the natives in parka coats when it is really nice out! Perception is reality. Pecans and pistachios are big, and my favorite place to eat is, appropriately, De La Vega's Pecan Grille. The Organ Mountains are a unique view from all over Las Cruces. Hike in Desert Peaks National Monument.—www.lascrucescvb.org.

New Mexico Farm & Ranch Museum, Las Cruces. Courtesy Barbe Awalt.

69. See the Art Collection at the Santa Fe Capitol Building

The most forgotten and overlooked major art collection in New Mexico is in the New Mexico Roundhouse —the State Capitol. Admission is free, and you can see wonderful contemporary and traditional art everywhere in all genres. Go to the Governor's Gallery to see shows of New Mexico's best. Parking is free but go when the legislature is not in session (January and February) because it is less crowded, you can park, and who wants to see a politician?—www.nmlegis.gov.

State Capitol Building, Santa Fe. Courtesy Barbe Awalt.

68. Walk Canyon Road

No matter the season, you need to visit Canyon Road in Santa Fe for the galleries, art, and experience. On Christmas Eve, there are bonfires, gay apparel, and singing. It is festive. Tourists and locals love to shop on Canyon Road.—www.visitcanyonroad.com.

Bill Hester Fine Art Gallery, Canyon Road, Santa Fe. Courtesy Barbe Awalt.

67. Experience a Matanza

Everyone loves pig and pork products. Matanzas were a way for a whole village to eat by slaughtering a pig—they are huge! It has been featured on Andrew Zimmern's *Bizarre Foods* TV show. The biggest Matanza of them all is the Valencia County Hispano Chamber of Commerce Matanza in Belen in January. We are talking over 17,000 people. There is an admission, but you can eat until you explode. We were judges one year when it was raining – not pretty. Warning: the kids may not want to see dead pigs carried on forklifts. Note: The Feds–USDA–tried to close the Matanza down because Matanzas in New Mexico don't have meat inspectors playing a major role. The Matanza won.—www.vchcc.com.

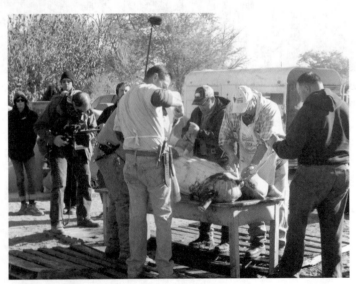

Birthday Matanza. Courtesy Barbe Awalt.

66. Drink a New Mexico Wine or Beer

Because of our climate, we are blessed with wonderful wines, rivaling California and Europe. The two best wine festivals are the Balloon Park Wine Festival and the Las Golondrinas Wine Festival. There is admission, and make sure you have a designated driver. I always have New Mexico sparkling wine (champagne) during the holidays.—www.nmwine.com.

There are some very good New Mexico beers, and they have won international awards. Have a drink!—www.nmbeer.org. By the way, there are good New Mexico tequilas too! Left Turn Distilling in Albuquerque makes a gin and a vodka, with rum and whiskey coming soon. —www.leftturndistilling.com.

Note: The Bernalillo Wine Festival unfortunately is no more. But the new Great Southwest Brew Fest featuring beers will be Labor Day weekend in Bernalillo.

Wines of New Mexico. Courtesy Barbe Awalt.

65. Go to a Gallery Opening

New Mexico does art—paintings, sculpture, textiles, ceramics, photography, folk art, religious art, lithographs, and more. Every village and town has galleries. The openings are fun. Meet an artist.

Santa Fe art gallery. Courtesy New Mexico True, New Mexico Department of Tourism.

64. Visit Bosque del Apache

See birds in wetlands. Go for the Festival of the Cranes at Bosque del Apache in November. You have two great choices for burgers in San Antonio—The Owl Cafe and the Buckhorn Tavern.—www.festivalofthecranes.com.

Visit an irrigation ditch and find out why acequias are so important to New Mexico life and culture. There are a lot of ditches to and from Bosque del Apache.—www.lasacequias.org.

And no, there are not pterodactyls overhead, but cranes and geese.

Bosque del Apache, San Antonio. Courtesy New Mexico True, New Mexico Department of Tourism.

63. Experience an Isotopes Game

There is nothing like it. Formerly the Dukes, the Isotopes (after the Simpson's TV show) have some of the highest Triple A baseball attendance in the country. Go during one of the many giveaways. It is good family fun. The Isotopes Park made the second edition of *101 Baseball Places to See Before You Strike Out* by Josh Pahigiam. The Isotopes are now part of the Colorado Rockies franchise.—www.milb.com.

Isotopes Stadium, Albuquerque. Courtesy Barbe Awalt.

62. Explore Taos

Taos is like going to another planet. They move slowly and appreciate the culture that Taos has through history. My favorites: Eskes Brew Pub, Millicent Rogers Museum, and shopping in the Plaza. Skiing is good during the winter. Embrace the Taos Hum and hum along.—www.taoschamber.com.

Go the fast way to Taos and come back on the High Road through Trampas and Truchas. This was where *Milagro Beanfield War* was filmed by Robert Redford. The scenery is breathtaking.—www.newmexico.org/high-road-to-taos-trail/.

Taos shops. Courtesy New Mexico True, New Mexico Department of Tourism.

61. Eat a Corn Product–Especially Blue Corn

Corn has been a staple in New Mexico for thousands of years. The Native Americans discovered it, and we enjoy it. Did you know we have blue corn? You haven't lived until you have blue corn pancakes, blue corn encrusted fish or chicken, or blue corn tortillas. You can buy corn mixes in the grocery store. Corn roasted on the cob is a big deal at festivals. Speaking of corn—Walker's Popcorn in Albuquerque, near UNM, has really fun flavors and great gifts to take home.—www.walkerspopcorn.com.

Bueno Posole. Courtesy Barbe Awalt.

60. Go to an Arts & Crafts Fair

Just like we love our art, we have tons of arts & crafts fairs—especially before the holidays. The biggest are: Weems, New Mexico Arts & Crafts Fair, Santa Fe Plaza Arts & Crafts Fair, and the Rio Grande Arts & Crafts Fair. Buy local and buy a charming one-of-a-kind item.—www.fairsandfestivals.net/state/NM/; www.craftsmasternews.com/newmexico.aspx.

Española Valley Arts and Crafts Fair, Española. Courtesy Barbe Awalt.

59. See the Albuquerque Sunport Art Collection

Another often over-looked "museum" of art is the Albuquerque Sunport Art Collection at the airport. Art is everywhere, and don't forget the art in the car rental facility. We are in a piece about Spanish Market in the car rental facility by Sylvia Martinez Johnson. Admission is free, but you have to pay to park. The Sunport was listed as #2 in Reader's Choice Best Airports for Art in *USA Today*.—www.cabq.gov.

Abstract Crown Dancer I *by Allan Houser, 2000, at the Albuquerque Sunport Rental Facility Complex. Courtesy Barbe Awalt.*

58. Stroll Old Mesilla

Old Mesilla, near Las Cruces, is like walking back into Old Mexico. The Plaza is casual, with a great church. Go in the shops or stop for a bite. Mesilla (Little Tableland) is the best-known and most visited historical community in Southern New Mexico. Museums in the small town include: Basilica of San Albino and the various walking tours. If you are there in October/November, see Dia de Los Muertos—Day of the Dead. May is the Cinco de Mayo Fiesta. My favorite places to eat are La Posta and St. Clair Vineyards Grill.—www.mesilla.com.

San Albino Church, Old Mesilla. Courtesy Barbe Awalt.

57. Buy a Ristra

Ristras are a time-honored tradition of weaving chiles into a long string. You can also buy wreath ristras. Ristras are traditionally red, but I have seen other colors. I have also seen plastic lights that look like ristras but without the dropage. That is why you want them outside.

Chile ristras. Courtesy New Mexico True, New Mexico Department of Tourism.

56. Wear a Broomstick Skirt or Bolo

A broomstick skirt is a staple for Native Americans, but Anglos love them, too. You can get short or long broomstick skirts of velvet, cotton print, or wool. Bolos for men or women have entered the world of fine art with a museum show and book. Bolos are so much more interesting than ties. Bolos can be made of anything from coinage, to precious stones, Native American pottery, art in miniature form, bone carvings, and precious metal. We have even seen them in computer parts by Marion Martinez. Did you know that Hispanic sheepherders in New Mexico used to carve bone bolos while they were tending to their flock? Bone carvings are made from horns of deer, elk, sheep, or goats.

Bolo tie collection. Courtesy Barbe Awalt.

55. Visit Gallup

Gallup is Indian Country. The galleries are great, but the pawn shops are even better. Do visit Red Rocks State Park. When in Gallup, visit the Zuni reservation. The Zuni are known for their silverwork and fetish carvings.—www.thegallupchamber.com.

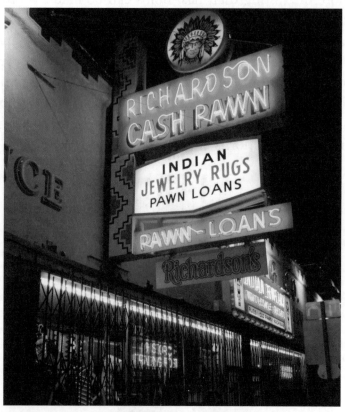

Richardson Pawn Shop, Gallup. Courtesy New Mexico True, New Mexico Department of Tourism.

54. See How Adobes Are Made

Adobes are bricks made of dirt, water, and hay. Then they are laid out in the sun to dry. It is an art that is all but forgotten. Cornerstones Partnerships in Santa Fe restores many old, adobe buildings in New Mexico. See how these necessary bricks are made. They have a history all over the world.—wwww.cstones.org; www.new-mexicoearth.com.

New Mexico Earth Adobes sign. Courtesy Barbe Awalt.

53. Explore Abiquiú Carefully

I say CAREFULLY because there is the sign at the entrance that is a bit intimidating. Be careful where you take pictures. The Abiquiú Inn is a great place to stay or eat in while touring. The Inn has a great gallery and store with local arts and crafts. Bode's Store is also a fun hangout with local color. Book in advance a tour for the Georgia O'Keeffe House. Did you know there are two major moradas as well as a picturesque church in Abiquiú? Take a short trip to Hernandez to see where Ansel Adams' famous picture was taken.—www.abiqui-uinn.com.

If you really love O'Keeffe art, check out the offerings at the O'Keeffe Museum in Santa Fe.—www.okeeffemu-seum.org.

Santo Tomás Church in Abiquiu. Courtesy Barbe Awalt.

52. Take a Soak

There are hot springs all over New Mexico. Ojo Caliente, Jemez Springs Bath House, and Ten Thousand Waves are the most famous, but there are so many more: All over Santa Fe, the Gila Hot Springs area, T or C area, Black Rock and Stagecoach in the Taos area, Montezuma Hot Springs on the campus of United World College in Las Vegas (New Mexico not Nevada), and others in the Jemez Springs area.—www.discovernewmexico.com/nmhotsprings/.

While in Jemez Springs, do visit a *caldera*—the center of a volcano. The Valle Caldera is huge, and has abundant wildlife and many recreation choices.—www.vallecalera.gov.

Jemez hot spring. Courtesy New Mexico True, New Mexico Department of Tourism.

51. Paint a Picture or Write a Book

Everyone in New Mexico can write a book, paint a picture, do crafts, create music, sculpt, or do something else artistic. I didn't say do it well, but everyone in New Mexico is creative. There is something about the light that makes people want to pick up a brush. Nurture your creative spirit. Take a class.

Courtesy Plein Air Painters of Southern New Mexico.

50. Visit Rio Rancho

The big Intel plant is front and center in Rio Rancho, but there is so much more. You can shop, eat, and check out new homes. You can go to an event at the Santa Ana Star Center. While in Rio Rancho, visit Corrales below. It is rumored to be the home of a mega number of wealthy people, but also it is a very old village that is very picturesque. Corrales has the dynamic twosome of the Historic Corrales Church and Casa San Ysidro across the street. It is especially worth seeing them if there is a festival.—www.rioranchonm.org.

Santa Ana Star Center, Rio Rancho. Courtesy Barbe Awalt.

49. Put Out Luminarias

Luminarias on Christmas Eve are a must. They are also called Farolitos in the north. They do bonfires at the Taos Pueblo. Luminarias are a way that many service groups or schools earn extra money for programs and, frankly, it is so much easier to have them do the work. Many families get together and have a luminaria party to make them or put them out. They can also be put out for parties and birthdays to be festive. There are electric versions too. Do not put lit candles on your roof!

Old Town Albuquerque has a beautiful display and it is part of the Luminaria Tour – sit on a bus, sing carols, and see great displays in the Country Club area and Old Town. Be warned, the Luminaria Tour sold out in a day the last few years.

Note: For the holiday season, do visit the River of Lights at the Albuquerque Bio Park near Old Town. There is a charge to see the lights.—www.cabq.gov/culturalservices/biopark.

Old Town luminarias, Albuquerque. Courtesy New Mexico True, New Mexico Department of Tourism.

48. Explore a Bosque

The Bosque in Albuquerque is famous, but there is a bosque anywhere there are rivers or creeks. The wildlife, bird-watching, and recreational activities are a long list. But when the fire danger is high, we all have to look out for fires and homeless camping in the bosques. Did you know that there are two towns south of Albuquerque—one called Bosque Farms and the other Bosque?

Bosque del Apache. Courtesy New Mexico True, New Mexico Department of Tourism.

47. Plant Vegetables & Fruits

The Native Americans had huge gardens, and there is a renaissance for home-grown veggies during our long growing season. The favorites? Chiles of all types, followed by squash, tomatoes, cilantro, corn, watermelons, grapes, and apricots. Go to a garden store and get authentic New Mexico seeds.—www.aces.nmsu.edu/pubs/_circulars/cr457/.

Farming pumpkins. Courtesy Barbe Awalt.

46. Visit a Film Set

Just follow the orange and black signs. TV shows, films, and music videos are filmed in New Mexico. All-calls are always in the papers or on TV. It is a hoot and you get paid, but make sure to take a book to read. It is a lot of sitting around but, who knows, you may see a film or TV star! Some of our books were used by a film company to make a fake bookstore set. Some came back with bullet holes. They reimbursed us.—www.newmexico.org/true-film/; www.nmfilm.com.

Movie sign for The Condemned II *(starring Wes Studi, Steven Michael Quezada, and Randy Orton) in Albuquerque. Courtesy Barbe Awalt.*

45. Go to a Lobo Game

The Pit is known as the loudest and most intimidating college basketball venue. See the Rio Grande Rivalry between UNM and NMSU in basketball. NOTE: The Pit was recently renamed WisePies Arena. Go figure. If you don't like basketball, do football, baseball, tennis, or soccer but not in the Pit.—www.golobos.com.

For the bowl fans, we now have the Gildan New Mexico Bowl in December. See football and all the accompanying activities. Gildan makes t-shirts and sportswear.—www.gildannewmexicobowl.com.

The Pit, Albuquerque. Courtesy Barbe Awalt.

44. Eat a Biscochito

The official New Mexico cookie is a *biscochito* (also spelled *bizcochito*). It is especially popular at the holidays. It comes in all shapes, and each baker has their own spin.—www.whatscookingamerica.net/cookie/biscochito.htm.

Way Out West Biscochitos. Courtesy Barbe Awalt.

43. Watch a Gunfight

Yup. We still have gunfights. Catch one in Old Town Albuquerque or other locations. We try not to use live ammo.—www.examiner.com/article/gunfighter-old-town.

Old Town Albuquerque gunfight. Courtesy James Blackburn, New Mexico Gunfighters Association.

42. Buy a Native American Pot

A Native American pot of any size is a treasure. Especially if you buy the pot on a visit to a Pueblo or the Navajo or Zuni Reservations. Second best, buy a Native American pot at Indian Market or some other festival. To be able to talk with the artist and even take a picture means you will have that memory for a long time. Ask permission first to take a picture of a Native American. Third best, buy a pot at a gallery. You have a lot of choices—buy a Native American pot!

Note: Native American pots in dirt are not there for the taking. Historic pots can sometimes be found in ruins or burial grounds on reservations. Remember the saying "Only take photos." Read about what is legal first.—www.atada.org; www.nmpots.com.

Outdoors Native American pot. Courtesy Barbe Awalt.

41. See Madrid

First of all, pronounce it correctly — not like the town in Spain — MAD-rid! It was founded in 1895 and has a colorful history. Madrid is on the Turquoise Trail, driving to Santa Fe, in a canyon in the Ortiz Mountains. It was a coal mining town near Cerrillos. It is very creative now with shops, festivals, a spa, museum, restaurants, art, a tavern, and a state park to hike. The town even had a AA Minor League baseball team with the Oscar Huber Ballpark, the first lighted ballpark west of the Mississippi in the 1920s. If you need a dose of funky—this is it. The movie *Wild Hogs* was filmed in Madrid.—www.visitmadridnm.com.

Madrid, New Mexico. Courtesy Barbe Awalt.

40. Drive on Juan Tabo in Albuquerque

No one knows who was Juan Tabo (pronounced Juan Ta Bó) and where the name came from. There are a few books on the road naming in Albuquerque, and it is a little slice of New Mexico history.

Juan Tabo street sign, Albuquerque. Courtesy Barbe Awalt.

39. Experience New Mexico Wind & Sun

When people tell me about the 50 mph wind at their house outside of New Mexico, I tell them we regularly have 60+ mph. We have learned to deal with it. It is bad for hair and contacts, and the dust is nasty. Maybe that is why we appreciate a nice day so much. We have sun almost all year—over 300 days. It makes this a great place to have solar and wind power. We installed solar at our home. We love it! The joke is, when you go swimming and get out of the pool, you will dry off instantly because of the wind. By the way, we have very little humidity. And if you have allergies, you will suffer in the spring; and if you don't have allergies, you will probably get some.

Macho Springs Wind Project. Courtesy Paul Rhetts.

38. Visit Los Alamos

The *Manhattan* TV show is hot now, though the locals say it is incorrect. Do visit Ashley Pond and Fuller Lodge. The Los Alamos Historical Society store has some publications that will help you understand the hilltop. Los Alamos has got a lot of secret stuff and some very smart people working there. Before you go to Los Alamos, view the *Manhattan* CD to get some background and the history. It may be flawed, but you do get insight on the "Hilltop."—www.visitlosalamos.org.

Fuller Lodge, Los Alamos. Courtesy Barbe Awalt.

37. See a Movie or TV Show Made in New Mexico

Breaking Bad, *Longmire*, *In Plain Sight*, *Wild Hogs*, *Manhattan*, and many more shows from the beginning of films and TV were filmed in New Mexico. You can tell you are near a set—follow the orange signs with cryptic black letters. Go to www.nmfilm.com to see how to list your property as a site and all kinds of other cocktail party tid-bits. You can find lists of what was done in New Mexico on the internet, but some lists are lacking and not current. We love standing-in for another state while the actual filming was done in New Mexico.

I-25 Studios, Albuquerque. Courtesy Barbe Awalt.

36. Cross the Rio Grande

I cross the Rio Grande a few times a week. I can see the level of the water or the trees along it turning colors. When you hot air balloon, pilots love to splash 'n dash in the river. Living only a mile away from the Rio Grande, I get to enjoy it all the time.

Rio Grande, southern New Mexico. Courtesy New Mexico True, New Mexico Department of Tourism.

35. Visit the Very Large Array

The Very Large Array is just cool. It has been in movies and is breathtaking. Is there someone out there? The Karl G. Jansky Very Large Array (VLA) was renamed in 2011. It is a radio astronomy observatory located about 50 miles west of Socorro. You can see it on U.S. 60.—www.public.nrao.edu/tours/visitvla.

Very Large Array, Plains of San Agustín. Courtesy NRAO/AUI and NRAO/AUI Photographer Bob Tetro.

34. Explore Ruidoso

Ruidoso is a real cowboy and Texas-like town. In spite of the Texas thing, it is a fun little town in the mountains. We have done four conventions there, so it is a popular destination to escape from the desert. If you visit in winter, visit Ski Apache. On the way to Ruidoso, I always get Carrizozo raspberry or cherry cider. You can get it at the grocery store in Ruidoso too!—www. skiapache.com, www.ruidosonow.com.

The Lincoln County Cowboy Symposium is held at the Ruidoso Downs Racetrack. There is music, food, poetry, authors, dancing, and the World Championship Chuckwagon Competition. You have seen the Competition on the Food Network with prizes over $13,000.— www.cowboysymposium.org.

Lincoln County Cowboy Symposium, Ruidoso. Courtesy New Mexico True, New Mexico Department of Tourism.

33. Go to a Ghost Town

Some say there are over 400 ghost towns in New Mexico. Some are used for film sets. Just make sure you have plenty of water! When mining was hot, there were gold towns, turquoise towns, silver towns, and even uranium towns. Now only a few are inhabited and working. Be careful because some of the buildings have been neglected for years, but they make great pictures. Be careful also of snakes. I hate snakes. But old buildings are wonderful places to live if you are a snake. Respect the privacy of people who live in and near old towns. Read about the towns and their history in many books on the subject.—www.vivanewmexico.com/ghosts/.

Steins, New Mexico, Ghost town. Courtesy Barbe Awalt.

32. Watch the Leaves Turn

We don't have leaves of all different colors like back East does, but the cottonwoods are an intense and beautiful golden yellow. The best place to see them is along the Rio Grande or any river. Fourth of July Canyon has a wonderful display in the fall.—www.takemytrip.com.

Aspens changing colors. Courtesy New Mexico True, New Mexico Department of Tourism.

31. Stand Outside & Taste Snow or Rain

We get rain or snow in New Mexico so rarely you have to enjoy it. Bathe in it! Drink it! Look at it! Take pictures of it! It is a desert, after all. When it snows, take a picture because the adobe in snow is just perfect! See a New Mexico TV weather person like Steve Stucker, Mark Ronchetti, or Joe Diaz for coming storms.—www. accuweather.com.

Albuquerque snow. Courtesy Barbe Awalt.

30. Visit a New Mexico Monument

We are blessed in New Mexico with some spectacular monuments. Every area has at least one. We have experienced snakes at Pecos Monument, hiked Bandelier, visited White Sands, visited Coronado, and many others.—www.nmmonuments.org.

Fort Selden State Monument. Courtesy of New Mexico True, New Mexico Department Tourism.

29. Take a Road Trip

Go from New Mexico and experience other states. We have been to California, Arizona, Colorado, Texas, and points east. We have never done Utah and have to do it. If you take a road trip, you can visit little places that are far off the main road. We have had some of the best meals in places that looked questionable but had lots of cars in front. Don't be put off by the name of the place. Joe's or Juan's may have great food.

Ghost Ranch. Courtesy New Mexico True, New Mexico Department of Tourism.

28. Get Caught in a Roadblock

Yes, we have gotten caught in roadblocks, and everyone should experience one! The first one I can remember was a DWI roadblock between Jemez Springs and Albuquerque with Father Tom Steele in the car. We have gotten in a few for weather, roadwork, and accidents. You can also get in one for escaped prisoners. Gives you time to talk and visit! Don't let prisoners in your car! Right before this book was published, I-25 in Valencia County was blocked because someone barricaded themselves in their car in the middle of the Interstate. We were there and saw it all. Drivers were not happy. The police shot him. End of story.—http://dot.nm.us.

Roadside DWI sign. Courtesy Barbe Awalt.

27. Ducks in Deming

Deming is in Southwestern, New Mexico, 33 miles from the Mexico border. Deming has been named a "Rock-Hunter's Paradise." The Deming Arts Center promotes the arts in Luna County. The Great American Duck Race in Deming has grown into a community-wide event with a parade, balloon rally, tortilla toss, slowpitch tournament, and of course the Duck Race.—www.demingduckrace.com.

Deming Duck Race. Courtesy New Mexico True, New Mexico Department of Tourism.

26. See New Mexican *Descansos* on Your Trip

Descansos are roadside memorials usually marking a place where a person lost their life. Usually *descansos* are created and maintained by family and friends of the departed. In New Mexico, you will see markers along roadsides. They can be very humble—just a cross—or ornate with ribbons, tinsel, and glitter. They can be of any material—plastic, wood, flowers, and with an inscription. Ghost Bikes are a form of *descanso,* usually a white bike marking the place where a biker died. Another oddity that may have a link to a family tragedy is decorated Christmas trees for the holiday. You can find them on medians. *Descansos* are protected by law; never treat them without reverence.—www.newmexicoexplorer.com/descansos.

Descanso *along I-25, south of Socorro, New Mexico. Courtesy Barbe Awalt.*

25. See New Mexico Animal & Bird Wildlife

We have a lot of wildlife—some not native. Of course you can see wildlife from a car—I saw lots of deer while travelling on I-25 going to Raton. But seeing wildlife from a hot air balloon is like being a voyeur. Check out the unusual and loud birds we have. Talk to your resident roadrunner.

If you like strange and bizarre—and who doesn't?—see the American International Rattlesnake Museum in Albuquerque. This is the place to take visitors who say they have seen it all. Where else can you see the largest collection of different rattlesnakes on exhibit in the world? It is on San Felipe NW, near Old Town, and there is an admission charge.—www.rattlesnakes.com.

Roadrunner (Geococcyx californianu), the New Mexico state bird.

24. Help Burn Zozobra

It is a mob scene, but do the Old Man Gloom event once. Burn your bad feelings when Zozobra goes up in flames. It is held in September every year in Fort Marcy Park in Santa Fe. The Burning of Zozobra event includes entertainment. Zozobra is over 50 feet tall, about 2,000 pounds, and made of: wood, wire, muslin, poultry netting, nails, screws, pulleys, plywood, shredded paper (all those bad thoughts to burn), spray paint, pizza pails, and duct tape. About 30,000 people attend the Burning of Zozobra. There is an admission charge, and you can get your tickets online.—www.burnzozobra.com.

Burning of Zozobra. Courtesy Kiwanis Club of Santa Fe.

23. Visit Tent Rocks

Tent Rocks are cool. How can you not be cool with HooDoos? It is a place you want to hike and respect the land. While there, get some Piki Bread. Kasha-Katuwe is on the Pajarito Plateau on Cochiti Pueblo south of Santa Fe. There is a charge to go into Tent Rocks.—www.explorenm.com/hike/tentrocks/.

Tent Rocks. Courtesy New Mexico True, New Mexico Department of Tourism.

22. Visit Roswell & Do Aliens

Roswell gives a whole new definition to crazy. The Roswell UFO Festival on the 4th of July is major, with thousands of people dressing up as aliens from space. Do go to the Roswell UFO Museum. Do bring your pet – they can dress up too. You can never have too much crazy.

See the New Mexico Military Institute, especially during formation.—www.roswellnm.org; www.roswellufo-museum.com.

Aliens. Courtesy New Mexico True, New Mexico Department of Tourism.

21. Explore Carlsbad

If you like bats, caverns, and going underground, you will love Carlsbad. The caverns and the bats are spectacular in Carlsbad Caverns National Park. Besides the caverns, Christmas on the Pecos is really different from anything else in New Mexico during the holiday season. There is also Brantley Lake and a whole lot of outside activities. You can smell the gas and oil production all around the Brantley Lake area. Make sure you visit the Living Desert State Park.—www.carlsbadchamber.com.

The Big Room, Carlsbad Caverns. Courtesy New Mexico True, New Mexico Department of Tourism.

20. Visit a Castle

Yes, we do have a magnificent castle in New Mexico —Montezuma Castle in Las Vegas. Historic Montezuma Castle became the home of United World College in 1982. The Castle started life in 1881 as a tuberculosis hotel and as a Harvey House. The Castle survived in spite of two fires, becoming a boxing training center in 1912, a Baptist college 1922 to 1931, a YMCA building, a Jesuit seminary 1937 to 1972, a set for the horror movie *The Evil*, and being forgotten. Tours are going to start of the Castle along with the refurbished Castañeda and Plaza Hotels. I had dinner in the grand room of the Castle, and it was elegant. Food was great. Sure, there were a couple hundred other people there, but it was still very nice.—www.uwc.org.

Montezuma Castle, Las Vegas. Courtesy Barbe Awalt.

19. Attend the Gathering of Nations

The Gathering of Nations Pow Wow in Albuquerque has over 500 tribes represented. The dances are beyond colorful. There is a Marketplace of Native American products. It is every spring and there is an admission charge.—www.gatheringofnations.com.

Grand Entrance, Gathering of Nations. Courtesy New Mexico True, New Mexico Department of Tourism.

18. Visit White Sands & Trinity Site

The Trinity Site, where the first atomic bomb was exploded in 1945, is open to the public two days a year, through the Stallion Gate entrance (from the north) or as an escorted caravan from the south from Tularosa High School—the first Saturday in April and the first Saturday in October (subject to change). White Sands is also worth seeing with its huge sand drifts. You can sled and ski down them. White Sands and Trinity Site are southeast of Albuquerque. Take food, water, a camera, and a photo id.—www.wsmr.army.mil/PAO/trinity.

White Sands National Monument. Courtesy New Mexico True, New Mexico Department of Tourism.

17. Retrace Route 66

Route 66 went from Chicago, Illinois, to Santa Monica, California. Experience the Mother Road in New Mexico. Stand on the corner of Route 66 and Route 66. Yes, because it was realigned in 1937, you can go to 4th Street and Central in Albuquerque and take a selfie. In Tucumcari there is a Texaco Gas Station on First Street that has continuously operated to the present. Do the Singing Road—WHAT? Yes, it is a stretch of road near Tijeras that plays "America the Beautiful" when you go the speed limit. Not kidding. It was even on TV—part of the National Geographic Channel's *Crowd Control* series!—www.rt66nm.org; www.abcnews.go.com/blogs/headlines/2014/10/route-66-adds-singing-road-as-speeding-deterrent/.

Old Route 66. Courtesy New Mexico True, New Mexico Department of Tourism.

16. Eat Pie in Pie Town

Of course you can order other things at the Pie-O-Neer Cafe, but you have to eat pie. Pie Town is a 2.5 hour drive from Albuquerque. There are two places to stay, a mercantile, RV park, and the Good Pie Cafe. When one pie café is closed, the other is open so do not fear —there is pie! Pie Town must have pie!—www.pio-neer.com; www.pietown.com.

Pies from Pie Town, New Mexico, 1940, by Russell Lee.

15. Whitewater in the Taos Box

In the spring, it is the thing to do if you are visiting the Taos area. Floating down the Rio Grande can be fun, wet, dangerous, or calm depending on the flow. Professional rafting companies have the correct equipment and know all the rules, especially how to stay safe. This would be a great place for a GoPro Camera. Visit the Taos Gorge Bridge.—www.highonadventure.com.

Rafting the Taos Box near the Taos Gorge Bridge, Courtesy Kokopelli Rafting Adventures, Taos.

14. Drink a Margarita

If you are going to have New Mexican food, you need a margarita to wash it down. There are all flavors, even non-alcoholic. There is even a Margarita Festival at Buffalo Thunder Resort! El Pinto has an extensive tequila bar and say they have the best margaritas, but a lot of places have the best—sample around? They do need to use fresh ingredients and not bottled stuff. I know my margaritas. Did you know we have tequilas that are made in New Mexico?

Santa Fe Margarita Mixes. Courtesy Barbe Awalt.

13. See the Tumbleweed Snowman

The Tumbleweed Snowman has now become a perennial favorite. The only thing better would be a Tumbleweed Snowlady too. You can only see the Snowman late November through December on I-40 in Albuquerque between the Carlisle and University exits on the north side. It is near the huge Native American pots on the median of I-40 that are also worth seeing. The Snowman started off small—3 to 4 feet—and now is huge. Don't stop on I-40 to see him—it is dangerous!!! It is a busy highway. You have to drive by and look. The Snowman is erected by Albuquerque Metropolitan Arroyo Flood Control Authority employees and has been in national magazines, media and, of course, local media. Occasionally it has to be pulled down for a day because of high winds. Be aware, other communities are now copying our Tumbleweed Snowman.—www.amafca. org/media/snowman.html.

The Tumbleweed Snowman, Albuquerque. Courtesy Barbe Awalt.

12. Mud Something

Yes, mud! We have dirt, so we in New Mexico have mud—just add water and some hay. Mudding is done periodically to moradas, churches, and even old houses. It is a way to cover over cracks and make everything new. You have to be invited to mud the penitente moradas in the north, but in Corrales they have mudding of the Old Church and are appreciative of all help. It is usually done when it is warm. You can meet some real characters doing it. Mudding is a perfect way to soften skin—it is a natural abrasive.—www.corraleshistory. com.

Mudding Abiquiú Morada. Courtesy Barbe Awalt.

11. Do Valentines Day in Lovington

Visit the Lea County Museum and get some cowboy vibes in Lovington. The Lea County Museum was created in 1969 by the Lovington Women's Club when they purchased the Commercial Hotel, which was about to be razed. The Lea County Museum is FREE and open except for Sunday. It is located at 103 South Love Street—a good reason to go there. You can also see the Western Heritage Museum & Lea County Cowboy Hall of Fame and Lea County ghost towns.—www.leacountymuseum.org.

Lea County Museum, Lovington, NM. Courtesy Jim Harris.

10. Read About New Mexico History

You have to understand New Mexican history. It was violent, mysterious, odd, colorful, and multi-cultural. There are a number of excellent New Mexico book publishers that specialize in New Mexico history. There is a wealth of books on New Mexico's history. Go and hear presentations from authors. The Historical Society of New Mexico Conference, every year, is a great place to start. It is held all over New Mexico—Las Cruces, Albuquerque, Santa Fe, Las Vegas, and many more cities. —www.hsnm.org.

9. Contribute to a Homeless Organization

Many people in New Mexico experience poverty. New Mexico is a poor state. Especially before Thanksgiving through Christmas there are food drives, clothes and coat drives, and special events. It is good to give back. Remember homeless animals too!—www. thestorehouseabq.org.

Roadrunner Food Bank of New Mexico has been serving the state since 1980. As the largest Food Bank in New Mexico, nearly 30 million pounds of food is distributed to four regional food banks and hundreds of partner agencies. Food is distributed to shelters, soup kitchens, pantries, group homes, low-income senior housing, and regional food banks. 70,000+ people receive food weekly through the Food Bank and its statewide partners. The Roadrunner Food Bank is also a member of Feeding America, the national network of the best food banks in America.—www.rrfb.org.

8. Visit Santa Fe

They say visit Santa Fe and buy in Old Town, but some things you can't find anywhere else. It is called the City Enchanted, Fantase, the City Different, the Theme Park, and it is unusual with many different people. A few things to see: any museum, the mysterious staircase at the Church of Loretto, Native American craftspeople under the portal at the Palace of the Governors, any arts festival, any place to eat, Golondrinas, and the views. My favorite places to eat right now are: Santa Fe Bite (used to be Bobcat Bite), Plaza Café (has a Southside location too), Mucho Gusto, The Shed for lunch, Saveur, Joe's, Midtown Bistro, Clafoutis French Bakery (parking is a struggle), and Harry's Roadhouse. If you have time, go to the Santa Fe Opera and get lost in the scenery outside the building. A day-long trip is to Museum Hill. A side trip to the Dixon Studio Tour, if it is open, is necessary. —www.santafe.org; www.santafeopera.org.

Santa Fe Plaza, looking toward the Palace of the Governors. Courtesy Barbe Awalt.

7. Buy Some Cowboy Boots

If you are in the West, you need boots. Short, tall, any color – so many boots. Sheplers, Cavender's, Boot Barn, Hillson's, KOWBOYZ, Back At The Ranch, and any flea market are all good choices—just go wild. You know that boots can protect you if you are attacked by a snake. Get a cowboy shirt too—look the part!

Santa Fe Flea Market boots. Courtesy Barbe Awalt.

6. Do the Santa Fe Indian Market

It is huge! Parking is practically gone, and overpriced if you can find it. Take the Rail Runner up, then the shuttle over to the Plaza. Just have fun seeing art, and eating Indian Tacos, and keep hydrated. There is jewelry, pots, art, fashions, sculptures, dolls, and much more. Indian Market starts with Preview the night before, and Indian Market goes for two days on the Santa Fe Plaza. The Indian Market takes place in August and was begun in 1922. There are many activities the two weeks before Indian Market.—www.swaia.org.

Award-winning artwork at Santa Fe Indian Market. Courtesy New Mexico True, New Mexico Department of Tourism.

5. Explore Albuquerque

There are so many places to see: ABQ Uptown, Downtown, The Heights, Old Town, North Valley, South Valley, West Side, UNM, CNM, and all the funky places in each. There is great food: Village Pizza on Rio Grande, Rt. 66 Diner (their milkshakes are to die for), Sadie's, El Pinto, Flying Star, and many more. Shop, go to a festival, see the Kimo Theater on Rt. 66, go to Expo/State Fair, see a museum, and just have fun. If you are an outside kind of person—HIKE! There are tons of things to do in the Bernalillo County Open Spaces. Who knows, you may meet Bernco Bernie. The Railyards are a new attraction on the weekends and have potential.—www. visitalbuquerque.org.

The Albuquerque Press Club began life in 1903, built by Illinois architect Charles Whittlesey as his home at 201 Highland Park Circle NE. It is very similar to one of his other designs, El Tovar Hotel at the Grand Canyon. —www.qpressclub.com/main/house-history.

The Kimo Theater, Albuquerque. Courtesy Barbe Awalt.

4. Shop Old Town

Old Town has recently become famous again for Blue Meth candy, inspired by *Breaking Bad*, at Candy Lady. If you like strange and bizarre—and who doesn't?—see the American International Rattlesnake Museum in Albuquerque. The best bookstore to buy New Mexico history and culture books is Treasure House Books on the Plaza. Do the luminarias in Old Town on Christmas Eve and the large Christmas tree for the Stroll in early December. There is even a Salsa Fest in Old Town. The Plaza and Gazebo have local color with weddings. The tours are great, including a ghost tour! San Felipe Neri Church is a photo magnet.—www.albuquerqueoldtown. com www.rattlesnakes.com.

Old Town shops. Courtesy New Mexico True, New Mexico Department of Tourism.

3. Eat a New Mexican Tortilla

Use a tortilla as bread, bake with it, and eat it for a snack. There are many flavors, including blue corn. Yes, there is even a red chile flavor. Put anything in a tortilla and it tastes good. There is nothing like a warm tortilla. There are imports from other states—make sure you get a New Mexico tortilla.

New Mexico Tortilla Company. By Barbe Awalt.

2. Visit Balloon Fiesta

It is the largest tourist event in New Mexico. Balloon Fiesta is the largest gathering of hot air balloons in the world. It is the most photographed event in the world. Balloon Fiesta is EARLY! Some tips: dress in layers, go early, take a bus if you can, tag your kids, bring plenty of money to eat and buy, take lots of pictures, and enjoy. Visit the Anderson-Abruzzo Albuquerque International Balloon Museum. If you see Chase Crews on the street trying to find their balloon, give them space. It is hard trying to find your balloon among 600 other hot air balloons. Locals all say publicly we are tired of hot air balloons and the traffic, but when the balloons go up it is the most beautiful thing you can see. Balloon Fiesta is in October, and there is an admission for most events.—www.balloonfiesta.com.

After Midnight balloon inflation. Courtesy Barbe Awalt.

1. Eat Red or Green Chile

The official New Mexico question is "red or green?"—chile! "Christmas" is red and green chile on your food. Know how to spell it—CHILE! There are many different kinds of chile—hot, mild, Sandia, decorative, ones large enough to stuff. By the way, red chile is mature green chile. It is grown in Chimayo, Socorro, and Hatch, but everyone in New Mexico has it in back-yard vegetable gardens. You can have chile wine, chile salsa of all kinds, chile candy, chile cookies, chile ice cream, and anything else you can think of. New Mexico is known for the Hatch Chile Festival, but chile festivals are now in all parts of New Mexico. Las Cruces boasts the Chile Pepper Institute. The Fiery Foods Show in early spring attracts thousands. I send New Mexico chile products to my friends and family for the holidays.—www.sos.state.nm.us/kids_corner/; www.chilepepperinstitute.org.

Hatch chile shop. Courtesy New Mexico True, New Mexico Department of Tourism.

Suggested Websites

www.newmexico.org/request-guide/ - to request a New Mexico guide

www.tripadvisor.com/tourism-g28952-New_Mexico-vacation.html

www.fodors.com

www.visitalbuquerque.org

www.tanm.org

www.bernco.gov

http://santafe.org

www.nmmagazine.com

www.planetware.com/tourist-attractions/new-mexico-usnm.htm

www.discoveramerica.com/usa/state/new-mexico.aspx

Rack of skulls. Courtesy New Mexico True, New Mexico Department of Tourism.

List of New Mexico State Symbols

Flag (1925)

Seal (1913)

Motto: Crescit eundo. It Grows as it Goes. (1887)

Nickname: Land of Enchantment or Tierra Encantado (1999)

Slogan: "Everybody is Somebody in New Mexico" (1975)

Question: "Red or Green" (1999)

Answer: "Red and Green" or "Christmas" (1999)

Capital: Santa Fe (1610)

English State Song: O Fair New Mexico (1917)

Spanish State Song: Asi Es Nuevo Mexico: Such is New Mexico (1971)

Bilingual State Song: Nuevo Mexico - Mi Lindo Nuevo Mexico, New Mexico – My Lovely New Mexico (1995)

Cowboy State Song: Under New Mexico Skies (2009)

State March: The New Mexico March

State Flower: Yucca Flower (1927)

State Tree: Two-Needle Piñon Pine (Pinus edulis) (1949)

State Grass: Blue Grama (Bouteloua Gracillis) (1973)

State Cookie: Bizcochito (1989)

State Vegetables: Chiles & Pinto Beans (Frijoles) (1965)

State Amphibian: New Mexico Spadefoot Toad (Spea Multiplicata) 92003)

State Animal: Black Bear (1963)

State Bird: Chaparral Bird (Greater Roadrunner) (1949)

State Butterfly: Sandia Hairstreak (2003)

State Fish: Cutthroat Trout (1955)

State Insect: Tarantula Wasp (Pepsis Formosa) (1989)

State Reptile: New Mexico Whiptail Lizard (Cnemidophorus Neomexicanus) (2003)

State Fossil: Coelophysis (1981)

State Gem: Turquoise (1967)

State Railroad: Cumbres & Toltec

State Necklace: Native American Squash Blossom

State Guitar: Pimentel New Mexico Sunrise Guitar (2009)

State Ballad: Land of Enchantment, Tierra del Encantada (1989)

State Poem: A Nuevo Mexico, To New Mexico (1991)

State Tie: Bolo (2007)

State Ships: USS New Mexico BB-40, USS New Mexico SSN-779 (1918-1946, 2008)

State Aircraft: Hot Air Balloon (2005)

New Mexico became the 47th State on January 6, 1912.

Plaza Hotel, Las Vegas. Courtesy Barbe Awalt.

The flag of New Mexico features the Zia Sun Symbol. The Zia Sun Symbol originated with the Zia Indians and has a stylized sun. The symbol has a circle with four points radiating outward. Four is the sacred number of Zia. The earth has four directions; there are four seasons. The day has four parts: sunrise, noon evening, and night; in life there are four stages: childhood, youth, manhood, and old age; and a man's four sacred obligations are: a strong body, a clear mind, a pure spirit, and devotion to the welfare of his people. Everything is bound together in the circle of life with love. There is no beginning or end. The Zia Sun Symbol is red on a background of Spanish yellow. The proportions of the Zia Sun Symbol are set by a legislative act.— www.sos.state.nm.us/Public_Records_And.../NMCentennialBlueBook.pdf

New Mexico State Flag. Courtesy Barbe Awalt.

Near Misses

We asked people on various social media channels to send in their best Bucket List entries. Here are some of them:

Visit El Morro National Monument – Crystal McClernon

Hike in Valles Caldera National Monument -- Melanie LaBorwit

Climb the cliff dwellings at Bandelier National Monument -- Melanie LaBorwit

Swim in summer at Soda Dam in Jemez River -- Melanie LaBorwit

Hike up Tree Spring trail in the Sandias for amazing views over Albuquerque -- Melanie LaBorwit

The American Flamenco Repertory Theater in Albuquerque with performances at the National Hispanic Cultural Center -- Barbe Awalt

Visit the miraculous painting in the rectory building just northeast of the Ranchos de Taos church -- Jaima Chevalier

Visit the hand-carved cave cathedral in northern New Mexico by Ra Paulette near Ojo Caliente -- Tomas Mas

Zip-line at 10,000' at Angel Fire -- Jim Tritten

Hike in the Sandia foothills at sunset -- ACVB

Visit the largest concave fresco in North America at the National Hispanic Cultural Center -- ACVB

Kayak the Rio Grande between Bernalillo and Alameda -- Paul Rhetts

Ride a bike across the ceiling at Explora -- ACVB

Go on a Breaking Bad location tour -- ACVB

Go to the Ty Murray Invitational Pro Bullriding Championship -- Paul Rhetts

Visit the Green Jeans Farmery, a new container development project, in Albuquerque near Carlisle NE & I-40 -- Barbe Awalt

Visit the old theater in Raton -- Jerry Hall

Visit the Vietnam Memorial in Angel Fire -- Jerry Hall

Hike the City of Rocks State Park between Deming and Silver City. Barbe Awalt

Scuba dive in the Blue Hole in Santa Rosa -- Jerry Hall

Poke around in downtown Socorro -- Jerry Hall

Give Lottery Scratchers for Christmas and birthdays—www.nmlottery.com -- Barbe Awalt

Sculpture of La Entrada by Sunny Rivera near the entrance of the Albuquerque Museum of Art & History. Courtesy Barbe Awalt.

TV & Films by Location

Some of the greatest tv shows and movies have been filmed in New Mexico. Here is just a sampling of some of them.

10 Years
2 Guns
2010
21 Grams
3:10 to Yuma

A Thief of Time
Ace in the Hole
Afterwards
All the Pretty Horses
Antiques Roadshow
Appaloosa
Armageddon
Around the Bend
As Cool as I Am
The Astronaut Farmer
Atomic Ed and the Black Hole
The Avengers

The Bachelor
Batman v Superman: Dawn of Justice
Beer for My Horses
Beerfest
Better Call Saul
Beyond the Blackboard
Bi the Way
Big Sky
Billy Jack

Bite the Bullet
Bless Me Ultima
Blood Father
Bobbie Jo and the Outlaw
Bobby Flay's Food Challenge
The Book of Eli
Bordertown
Born Innocent
Breaking Bad
Brokeback Mountain
Brothers
The Burning Plain
The Burrowers
Butch Cassidy and the Sundance Kid

Casey's Shadow
City Slickers
Clockers
Comancheria
The Comeback Trail
Conspiracy
Contact
Convoy
Cowboy
Cowboy del Amor
The Cowboys
Cowboys & Aliens
Crash

Crazy Heart
Cruel World

Dark Country
Dead Man's Burden
Diners, Drive Ins & Dives
Dirty Weekend
Dogs of War
Due Date

Easy Rider
Elvis Has Left the Building
Employee of the Month
Every Which Way but Loose
The Eye

Fanboys
Felon
First Snow
Five Days from Home
Five Dollars a Day
The Flock
Fort Bliss
Frank
Fright Night
Frontera

Gamer
Gas Food Lodging
Gas-s-s-s
The Gatling Gun
Georgia O'Keeffe
Ghosts of Mars
Goats
Gold
Good Kill

Good Morning America
The Grapes of Wrath
The Guest

Hamlet 2
Hang 'Em High
Heaven with a Gun
The Hi-Lo Country
The Hitcher
The Homesman
The Host
House of Cards

In a Valley of Violence
In Dreams
In Plain Sight
In the Valley of Elah
Independence Day
Independence Day: Resurgence
Indiana Jones and the Kingdom
    of the Crystal Skull
Indiana Jones and the Last
    Crusade
Infinity
Intruders
Iron Man 2

Jane Got a Gun
Jarhead
John Carter
Jonathan Livingston Seagull
Journey to the Center of the
    Earth
The Juror

Katie Says Goodbye
Kickboxer 4
The Killer Inside Me
Killer Women
King Solomon's Mines
Kites
Kites: The Remix

The Legend of the Lone Ranger
Legion
Lemonade Mouth
Let Me In
Lewis and Clark and George
Little Miss Sunshine
Little Treasure
Lolita
The Lone Ranger
Lone Survivor
Lonely Are the Brave
Lonesome Dove
The Longest Yard
Longmire
Lust in the Dust

MacGruber
Mad Love
The Man from Laramie
The Man Who Fell to Earth
Manhattan
The Men Who Stare at Goats
The Messengers
The Milagro Beanfield War
A Million Ways to Die in the
    West
The Missing
The Muppet Movie

My One and Only

Natural Born Killers
The Night Shift
Nightwing
No Country for Old Men
North Country
Not Forgotten

Observe and Report
Odd Thomas
Off the Map
Outrageous Fortune

Paper Heart
Paul
Persecuted
Powwow Highway
Private Lessons
The Prodigal Planet

Red Dawn
Red Sky at Morning
Rent
The Resident
Rounders
Route 66

Save Me
Second Thoughts
Seraphim Falls
Shot Caller
Sicario
The Signal
Silkwood
Silverado

Spare Parts
Sparks: The Price of Passion
The Spider
The Spirit
Spoiled
The Spy Next Door
Sundown
Sunshine Cleaning
Superman
Suspect Zero
Sweetwater
Swing Vote

The Taliban Shuffle
Tank Girl
The Tao of Steve
Tennessee
Terminator 2: Judgment Day
Terminator Salvation
Them!
This Must Be the Place
Thor
Three Wise Guys
Timerider: The Adventure of Lyle Swann
Tortilla Heaven
Trade
Traffic
Transcendence
Transformers

Transformers: Revenge of the Fallen
True Grit
Twins
Two Men in Town
Two-Lane Blacktop

Undead or Alive

Vacation
Vampires

Walker, Texas Ranger: Last of a Breed
The War Boys
War on Everyone
We're the Millers
White Sands
Wild Hogs
Wild Wild West
Wildfire
Wisdom
Wyatt Earp

X-Men DOFP: Rogue Cut

Year One
Young Guns
Young Guns II

Build Your Own Bucket List

1.
2.
3.
4.
5.
6.
7.
8.
9.
10.
11.
12.
13.
14.
15.
16.
17.
18.
19.

20.

21.

22.

23.

24.

25.

26.

27.

28.

29.

30.

31.

32.

33.

34.

35.

36.

37.

38.

39.

40.

41.

42.

43.

44.

45.

46.

47.

48.

49.

50.

51.

52.

53.

54.

55.

56.

57.

58.

59.

60.

61.

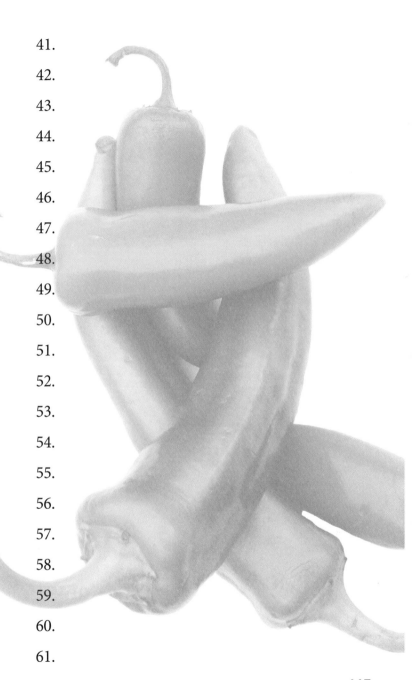

62.

63.

64.

65.

66.

67.

68.

69.

70.

71.

72.

73.

74.

75.

76.

77.

78.

79.

80.

81.

82.

83.

84.

85.

86.

87.

88.

89.

90.

91.

92.

93.

94.

95.

96.

97.

98.

99.

100.

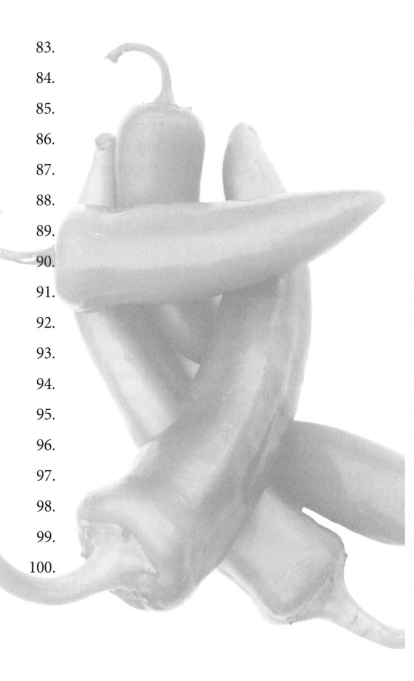

Roadrunner Food Bank

Roadrunner Food Bank of New Mexico has been serving the state since 1980. Roadrunner Food Bank was founded by Reverend Titus Scholl. He started by distributing food to the hungry from the trunk of a car. Thirty years later the mission has stayed the same—feed the hungry in our community.

As the largest food bank in New Mexico, nearly 30 million pounds of food is distributed to four regional food banks and hundreds of partner agencies. Food is distributed to shelters, soup kitchens, pantries, group homes, low-income senior housing, and regional food banks. 70,000+ people receive food weekly through the Food Bank and its statewide partners. The Roadrunner Food Bank is also a member of Feeding America, the national network of the best food banks in America. One of their annual public events is just before Super Bowl weekend called Souper Bowl.

Information about Roadrunnner Food Bank: www.rrfb.org. Office: 5840 Office Blvd. NE, Albuquerque, NM 87109. Donate on the website, with food, or send a check. To volunteer: 505/247-2052. Questions? info@rrfb.org.

ABOUT THE AUTHOR

Barbe Awalt is an author, publisher, photographer, and is passionate about New Mexico. She won the Mother Teresa Award, with husband Paul Rhetts, for their work promoting Hispanic New Mexican art. She and her husband have published some of the best books about New Mexico.

Geronimo Springs Museum, Truth or Consequences. Courtesy Barbe Awalt.